PROSPERITY FOUNDATION

Book One of a Five Book Series

Experience God's Foundational Truths for Prosperity Through the Power of God's Word

by
Valerie Rogers

Unless otherwise indicated, all scripture quotations are taken from the *King James Version* **of the bible.**

Prosperity Foundation, Book One – Experience God's Foundational Truths for Prosperity Through the Power of God's Word
ISBN 1-59581-230-X
Copyright © 2005 by Valerie Rogers
Checed Publications, LLC
1282 Smallwood Drive West, #125
Waldorf, Maryland 20603-4732

Printed by:
Brentwood Christian Press
4000 Beallwood Avenue
Columbus, Georgia 31904
United States of America.
www.BrentwoodBooks.com

All rights reserved under International Copyright Law. Contents and/or cover may not be *reproduced* in whole or in part in any form without the express written consent of the author.

Contents

Acknowledgments 4

Preface 6

Foreword 8

Chapter 1   Introduction: God's Divine Plan 11

Chapter 2   Pain – An Indicator of Disorder 13

Chapter 3   God's Divine Purpose for Man 14

Chapter 4   The Void Only Jesus Can Fill 16

Chapter 5   God's Mandate and Purpose 17

Chapter 6   The First River – Pison: 20

Chapter 7   The Second River – Gihon:. 23

Chapter 8   The Third River – Hiddekel:. 25

Chapter 9   The Forth River – Euphrates: 26

About the Author 27

Acknowledgments

Trust in the Lord with all thine heart, lean not unto thine own understanding. In all thy ways acknowledge Him, and He shall direct thy paths. Proverbs 3:5-6

First of all, Lord, I acknowledge You, for you have directed my path to put to paper the words You want declared in the earth. I feel as David did when he asked, "What is man that You are mindful of him?" I acknowledge you, Lord, for You have ordered my steps and brought me to this place in You. For the times when I said, "There was no God, for He is dead.", You still watched over me and protected me–keeping death and destruction from getting too close to me. For the times when I did lean to my own understanding and to my own devices, You extended your mercy towards me. For the times when I just wanted to shut down and give up, when I wouldn't believe You and instead believed the deceptions of the enemy and trusted in the frailties of man, You were longsuffering with me and continued to express Your love for me. For the times when I ran from Your call upon my life, You waited patiently and did not give up on me.

I acknowledge you, Lord, for connecting me–by covenant–to a spiritual father: Bishop Elect Rodney S. Walker, Sr. He is a Senior Prophet indeed who nurtures and fine-tunes me by pouring into my life and by challenging me in the way of the prophetic.

I acknowledge Your grace, Lord, in helping me to endure the wilderness journey and process. I thank You for every person that's been placed in my life along the way. Whether they meant me good or harm does not matter because it all works for my good.

I love You, Lord, and I acknowledge that all of this is according to Your purpose for my life–a time such as this!

Lord, I know you're not done perfecting me yet, for the process continues until Your return!

Preface

I am so delighted that my spiritual daughter has written on this subject. I believe that she has tapped into something that will drastically change the very life of each person who will endeavor to read, hear and do what is written in this series of books.

As people of God, it is imperative that we tap into what God is doing in this time. We have entered a season where God is doing the kinds of things that people of old never had the chance to experience. Anyone that really connects with what God is financially doing in this time will experience a supernatural harvest that so many others have only dreamt of. This is certainly a "Season of Opportunity".

Valerie has received a revelation that will make a tremendous impact upon the body of Christ. We must realize that God is looking for people who will take His word and run with the understanding that He wants to bless them immensely. When God says things like, " I will bless thee coming in and I will bless thee going out" and "Whatsoever you do shall prosper", I know that He is up to something that will bless us in our time.

As prophets, we have understanding of seasons and times and this is one of the seasons that the body of Christ must embrace. Valerie is very conscious of this being the time and season that God has chosen to bless his people. She has mentioned, in her writings, so many things that are proven revelation; but if we miss the fact that order, character, and integrity are key components, we will miss the whole point of prosperity. If you really want to please God and to be prosperous, become people of integrity who are totally submitted to order.

As you read these powerful books, it is my prayer that you will be as those to whom the words of Revelation 1: 3 are directed: "Blessed is he that readeth, and they that hear the words of this prophecy, and keep those things which are written therein: for the time is at hand."

May the Lord bless you richly,
Prophet Rodney Walker, Sr.

Foreword

Christ is soon to return and the signs will be:

> *... Ye shall hear of wars and rumors of wars, be ye not troubled: for such things must needs be; but the end shall not be yet. For nation shall rise against nation, and kingdom against kingdom; and there shall be earthquakes in diverse places and there shall be famines and troubles: these are the beginnings of sorrows. Mark 13:7-8.*

God is looking for a readied people–a body of believers that is chaste and pure, without spot or wrinkle. According to the book of Acts, chapter 3, verses 20 and 21, *heaven must receive Him until the times of restoration of all things which God has spoken by the mouth of all His holy prophets since the world began.*

Restoration means *back again; to restore as to health or soundness. To restore lost dominion or authority; restoring a thing back to its former condition.* Our former condition is described in the book of Genesis, chapter one: "In the beginning...". God created man in their (the plurality of the Godhead) image and after (according to the nature of) their likeness.

> *And God said, Let us make man in our image, after our likeness: and let them have dominion over the fish of the sea, and over the fowl of the air, and over the cattle, and over all the earth, and over every creeping thing that creepeth upon the earth. Genesis 1:26*

According to verse 28, God blessed man and said unto **them**, (not him), **be** fruitful, and multiply, and replenish the earth, and subdue it: and **have dominion**...

There is a transfer taking place. It is a transfer of authority, of wealth, of soundness of mind, and of prosperity (bringing back into manifestation the original order given unto man)–"having dominion." This dominion can only be accomplished through Jesus Christ who was our earthly example for walking according to the principles of the Kingdom of God.

These books were written through the inspiration of the Holy Spirit to, first: proclaim the gospel of the Kingdom of God and His mandate for us to be restored to our place of having dominion. Dominion cannot be nor will it ever be accomplished except through abiding in Christ and by the power of the Holy Spirit.

Those who have ears to hear, let them hear; and those who have eyes to see, let them see what is taking place in this hour. A shift towards kingdom dominion is becoming more apparent. We must be a prepared people, sent by God, to preserve posterity in the earth and to save lives by a great deliverance.

> *For as in the days that were before the flood they were eating and drinking, marrying and giving in marriage, until the day that Noe entered into the ark, And knew not until the flood came, and took them all away; so shall also the coming of the Son of man be. Matthew 24:38-39*

Many of God's people will become deceived and ultimately lost if we do not take heed to the times and prepare ourselves. The time has come to prepare, work and store while it is yet day–for night cometh, when no man can work (John 9:4).

> *Go to the ant, thou sluggard; consider her ways, and be wise: Which having no guide, overseer, or ruler, provideth her meat in the summer, [and] gathereth her food in the harvest. Proverbs 6:6-8*

We have a guide: His name is the Holy Spirit who guides us into all truth (John 16:13). We have an overseer who is the set gift in the house of worship where God has set each of us–our wealthy place. We have a ruler; His name is Jesus Christ–the King of kings and the Lord of lords. In accordance with how we were divinely created for His purpose, we too are kings and lords. Our time to pluck up that which has been planted is now. For the harvest is plenty and the laborers few. This statement applies not just in evangelizing lost souls, but also in gathering and storing the wealth that is being transferred from the wicked to the just. We need to consider the ways of the ant otherwise we will not survive the next season.

Prophet Valerie Rogers, September 2005

Chapter 1

Introduction: God's Divine Plan

There was once a time when man decided to build a city and a tower whose top would reach unto heaven, making a name for themselves. They were one people. They were all of one language. This was the beginning of what they could do. God considered that there was nothing they imagined they could do that would be impossible for them (Genesis 11:4, 6). At this point, man was being according to his divine nature but not according to God's divine plan. God could not allow these persons to fulfill their goal because it was contrary to His divine plan for man–to be fruitful, and multiply, and replenish the earth. Additionally, God could not allow them to fulfill their plan because they purposed to make a name for themselves and they were not doing what they were doing to glorify God. So He confounded their language and scattered them abroad unto the face of the whole earth until it was time for His divine plan to be fulfilled in the death, burial and resurrection of Jesus Christ. It was on the day of Pentecost that God brought man together again as one through the baptism of the Holy Spirit in order for man to build His kingdom in the earth.

It is the apostles and prophets who lay the foundation–Ephesians 2:20. With Christ as the chief cornerstone, all things as it pertains to the Kingdom of God and the principles of living prosperously must be built upon Him. *Except God builds the house, they that labor, labor in vain* (Psalm 127:1).

You may wonder, "What does that have to do with financial prosperity and abundance?" As a born-again Christian, unless your spiritual life is built upon the principles of Christ and the Kingdom of Heaven, what you have labored to do is in vain.

Remember the parable of the house that was built? One was built upon solid rock, the other upon sand. When the strong winds and storms came, the one built upon sand could not stand. Moreover, let's also consider the cost of building. If you were to lose everything, could you build again? It would be difficult to rebuild unless the foundation of everything you did was built upon kingdom principles.

But you say, "I'm standing on pretty solid ground. I have a good income, a home, cars and my family is well off. I even have money set aside for emergencies." Praise God! I don't mean to alarm you, but we are probably living in the most challenging times of our lives. If you failed to build upon sound principles, would you be able to recover should you have a potential "Job" experience?

Let's look at Job's life. He was very prosperous. He loved God, served God and served the community. God even said that there was none like him in all the earth. Well, what happened?

With all of the prosperity that was evident in Job's life, there was still something outside of God's order that hindered Job from advancing to the next level in God. God permitted Satan access to exploit what was out of order in Job's life and to bring him (Job) into alignment with God's divine plan and purpose.

Chapter 2

Pain–An Indicator of Disorder.

Pain is an indicator that something needs to be brought back into order–according to God's original design and purpose.

What comes out of you when the pressure is on? Do you ignore a situation in hopes that it will miraculously go away? Do you worry about it?

How do you mask your pain? Do you do it through smoking, drinking, overspending or some other addiction? Remember, when pain shows up there is something out of order that God is trying to restore. God's objective is for us to have peace and to have it more abundantly–nothing missing or lacking–absolute wholeness and soundness. Most people do not have total peace because they are not walking in the fullness of God's original design and purpose. Outside of relationship with God, there is no peace. We cannot have peace without God.

> *Thou wilt keep [him] in perfect peace, [whose] mind [is] stayed [on thee]: because he trusteth in thee. Isaiah 26:3*

When pain is present, there is something missing or lacking; there is no total peace. God wants to restore us to a place of total peace and that can only be done through understanding that God has a divine order for all that He's created. Anything outside of that order is not whole or sound.

Chapter 3

God's Divine Purpose for Man

Without understanding who we are according to God's specifications and purpose for our lives, we can never be in divine order.

What do I mean when I say that things are out of order? According to <u>Merriam Webster Dictionary</u>, *order* is defined as:

- rank, class or special group
- arrangement
- rule of law
- authoritative regulation or instruction
- working condition
- special request for a purchase or what is purchased

Genesis 1:28 describes God's mandate and purpose for man.

> *And God blessed them, and God said unto them, **Be fruitful**, and **multiply**, and **replenish the earth**, and **subdue it:** and **have dominion** over the fish of the sea, and over the fowl of the air, and over every living thing that moveth upon the earth.*

Whenever there is pain in our lives, we're not functioning in God's divine purpose. Pain is an indicator that something is not working according to its original specifications. Man was made in the image of God and enjoyed fellowship with Him in the garden in the cool of the day. Not only were we designed to enjoy fellowship and relationship with God or to be in harmony with His purpose for us, His original specifications for us, were according to His image and after His likeness.

Man had an assignment. When God positioned man in his assignment (NOTE: God set man in the garden after God finished His creative work.), man's reward was continued fellowship with

God. Out of all that God created in the universe, His desire was to fellowship on a regular basis with man. God came to fellowship with man. We're talking about an all powerful, all knowing God who created everything including man, came down to spend time with His creation. Yet when Adam sinned by disobeying God, he lost his position of fellowship and his reward.

If you ever come to a place of enjoying the presence of God and then suddenly it is no more–you will find yourself in a very painful situation. Even David asked the Lord, in Psalm 51:11, to not cast him away from His presence or take His Spirit from him. David enjoyed the presence of God, but something out of order in his life caused him to risk losing his position of fellowship with God.

So, pain is an indicator that something is not in its proper order. God sent His only begotten Son to restore order. As you received Him as Savior and Lord, that was the beginning of bringing everything within you back to its original design and purpose.

> *Therefore if any man be in Christ, he is a new creature: old things are passed away; behold, all things are become new. 2 Corinthians 5:17*

We see in the 3rd chapter and the 25th verse of the book of Job that Job, himself, realizes and confesses that fear was the door that allowed the enemy to walk right in and bring havoc to his life. Now, some would say that it was God who gave Satan permission to turn Job's world upside down. But Job was living a prosperous life. He had a hedge of God's protection around him; yet, God knew there was disorder in his life.

Satan presented a sound argument which gave him legal access to Job. Sure, he was not authorized to take Job's life; but he could bring pain and suffering to him through disorder.

Chapter 4

The Void Only Jesus Can Fill

Think about what brought you to the reality of needing Christ in your life, if you are saved. Or, think about the feeling of voidance and emptiness that you try to fill in your life from time to time. You know—that dull ache that is down in the pit of your stomach. It could be the pain of loneliness, the pain of rejection, the pain of abuse or the pain of inadequacy. These are indicators that there is an emptiness within you that longs to be filled. That emptiness can only be filled with Jesus Christ. That place is reserved for Him.

When you said, "Jesus, I believe you died for me so that I can live", He immediately took His position in your life and heart and began to manifest the process of restoring you back to who you were created to be.

Sin brought forth disorder and disunity. Jesus dying on the cross for our sin brought forth the manifestation of order and unity.

Chapter 5

God's Mandate and Purpose

Let's go back to the book of Genesis:

> *And the Lord God **planted** a garden eastward in Eden; and there He put the man whom He had formed. And out of the ground made the Lord God to grow every tree that is pleasant to the sight, and good for food; the tree of life also in the midst of the garden, and the tree of knowledge of good and evil. And a river went out of Eden to water the garden; and from thence it was parted, and became into four heads. The name of the first is **Pison:** that is it which compasseth the whole land of Havilah, where there is gold; And the gold of that land is good: there is bdellium and the onyx stone. And the name of the second river is **Gihon:** the same is it that compasseth the whole land of Ethiopia. And the name of the third river is **Hiddekel:** that is it which goeth toward the east of Assyria. And the fourth river is **Euphrates. And the Lord God took the man, and put him into the garden of Eden to dress it and to keep it.** Genesis 2:8-15*

As you can see, according to the book of Genesis, the Lord God planted a garden and placed the man He created into that garden to work. His responsibility was to dress it and to keep it for the Lord. Within his place of purpose, wealth and everything pleasant to eat was provided. He lacked nothing. God even gave him suitable help to assist him.

Upon planting the garden, there was also a river that watered the garden. This river was parted and became four heads. In the garden where God places you to dress it and keep it, the river symbolizes a life giving force which becomes four heads. Each of these heads represents a separate income stream. The pattern shown here indicates that when we are in the place God prepared for us, there will be four streams of income to sustain that over which He has given us charge.

Always remember that God created us with a purpose in mind. You cannot bear fruit and multiply without the proper conditions being met.

First, the following condition must be met: The place that you are in must be a place God created specifically for you. This place will already be in existence when He puts you there.

Second, you must be willing to be obedient and "to go". The place He created for you may not be what you had in mind, but I believe that at some time in your life you were given an indication of what that place would be. You were created to solve a problem. What do you love doing the most? Let me help you respond appropriately to this question by this determining factor: You will know what you love if it is something you have a desire to do even if you never get paid for doing it. That is an indication that you have a passion for doing it. If you have a passion, then more than likely there is a group of people who will pay you and celebrate you for that passion.

Too often we are driven by other influences which determine what we should do. Those things could be far from what God purposed for our lives. Riches and wealth do not always equate to dollars and cents. More times than we care to admit, we get caught up in pursuing someone else's dream that was imposed upon us. We do so either because we don't realize that the imposition is actually taking place, or because we are not comfortable with who we are and we are trying to please someone else. It may also be because we have felt that we didn't have many choices available to us. Limited choices could be the result of the amount or lack of education we have, social barriers or other misfortunes in our lives.

I pray this will set you free today, for God knew what He had in mind for you before you were formed in your mother's womb. Life's circumstances have not changed what God predetermined. He created you with purpose and greatness in mind. I recall, as a young child, having a desire to teach. As I was growing up and throughout part of my adult life, I got away from that desire–pursuing what I thought would bring in a larger income. But, God is so faithful! When I turned my heart back to Him, He provided various common and uncommon ways for me to exercise my gift and my love for teaching. He continues to expand my capacity to do so even today.

Third, when you are in the right place there will be streams or rivers of water to sustain you in the place where God set you. In the following four chapters, we will take a look at each of these rivers.

Chapter 6

The First River–Pison:

The name of the first river is Pison; it compasses the whole land of Havilah where there is gold. The gold of that land is good. Pison in Hebrew means "increase". Imagine that the first thing God does upon setting you in your place is to begin a process to bring about increase. Havilah, however, symbolizes suffering pain, which brings forth. In order to come into the increase God has for you, you will suffer through some things. Often, the process of restoration will be painful because our thinking has to be changed, our outlook has to be changed and how we manage the things of God has to be changed and accomplished according to His divine specifications.

Consider, in the natural, a woman who is bringing forth a child. Prior to the child coming forth out of her womb, there is pain, pressure and suffering. But at the birth of the child, at the time of delivery, the woman brings forth **the increase** of her lineage through that child.

> *A woman when she is in **travail** hath sorrow, because her hour is come: but as soon as she is delivered of the child, she remembereth no more the anguish, for joy that a man is born into the world. John 16:21*

According to the word in Genesis chapter 2, there is gold in the land of Havilah and the gold of that land is good. God, Himself declares the gold in that land as good. The gold often symbolizes the glory of God–the 'kabowd', or splendor of God. It is very precious. In other words, the gold or glory is not common. A price must be paid, through suffering, to receive that kind of increase.

> *For our light affliction, which is but for a moment, worketh for us a far more exceeding [and] eternal weight of glory; 2 Corinthians 4:17*

In order to receive the increase of God's abundance, there must be a process of bringing us–our mind, will and intellect–into alignment with the will of God and into His way of thinking. He does that so we are able to produce lasting, "kingdom-oriented" fruit. What God teaches us will enable us to produce consistently and skillfully lasting, eternal results. For the things of God are eternal. The things we learn of this world are not.

> *Enter ye in at the strait gate: for wide [is] the gate, and broad [is] the way, that leadeth to destruction, and many there be which go in thereat: Matthew 7:13*

God makes the place of purpose before He makes the man. He brings or sets him in that place to dress (work) it and to keep it. This principle is seen in the book of Genesis where God creates the Garden of Eden first, and then he places the man whom He made in His own image and after His likeness. God created man and then breathed upon Him to do the work He purposed for him to do: To be fruitful, to multiply, to replenish, to subdue and to have dominion. In the New Testament, Jesus also breathed upon man–His disciples, and commanded them to go forth and do the work they were purposed to do (John 20:22).

God's divine order is for each of us to receive the maximum manifestation of His purpose and promise. In the natural, setting a broken bone so that it can properly heal is a painful process because the bone may have to be set into proper alignment before the process of healing and restoration takes place. As it is in the natural, so it is in the spiritual. There are areas of brokenness in our lives: unforgiveness, rejection, anger, offense, addictions, and the like–all of which are used to serve as insulators–shielding our issues from feeling pain. God must break down these barriers in order to get to the root of the issue. Spiritual Surgery must be performed to remove the growth so that healthy tissue will be able to live and thrive. Once healing and restoration takes place, we are no longer affected by these issues or infecting others with them.

By looking at the patterns in God's word, you will see there is pain and suffering before the bringing forth of His increase. However, Jesus declares there is joy at the end of the process.

> *For His anger endureth but for a moment; in His favour is life: weeping may endure for a night, but joy cometh in the morning. Psalm 30:5*

Havilah also symbolizes region. This means that God has prescribed an area, region or land for you to possess. After the process of equipping and preparing you for increase has taken place so that God's glory is revealed, an endowment to work the land we are set in is released.

Chapter 7

The Second River–Gihon:

The name of the second river is Gihon which symbolizes the "valley of grace". God will provide grace in your process to dispossess. He gives you the land, but just as He commanded Adam, so must we also work to dress and maintain the land wherein He has set us.

The same principle is shown in Genesis 13 where God shows Abraham the land He had given unto Abraham's seed to possess forever. Yet in chapter 15, God indicated that the land and the people must be prepared before they could go in and fulfill their purpose. If you recall: Abraham's seed, the children of Israel, suffered through bondage in Egypt and were tested in the wilderness before God felt they were ready to go in and possess the land He promised to them. They eventually entered the land, but they were required to work it to make it fruitful. Here are some observations to consider:

- God provided grace in their victory to dispossess. Likewise, He will also provide us with grace to overcome.
- Israel was disobedient and didn't dispossess all. Those who remained were used by God to prove the children of Israel. If we don't learn to overcome our circumstances, our circumstances will overcome us and continue to buffet us as thorns in our sides.
- Israel could have taken as much land as they could handle. We, too, can have more than enough if we're willing to pay the cost.

Gihon also symbolizes "bursting forth".

> *Enlarge the place of thy tent, and let them stretch forth the curtains of thine habitations: spare not, lengthen thy cords, and strengthen thy stakes; For thou shalt break*

> *forth on the right hand and on the left; and thy seed shall inherit the Gentiles, and make the desolate cities to be inhabited. Isaiah 54:2-3*

God is a progressive God and in order to increase your territory, there must come times of trials and testings. However, in the end you will have your breakthrough–a time of breaking out of what seems like containment into greater realms of your purpose and destiny. You have demonstrated that God can trust you with His riches to establish His covenant in the earth. When you are shown faithful over a little, then He will make you a ruler over much.

But you say, "Wait a minute, don't I have a lot when I am at Havilah where the gold is good?" Keep in mind, God's thoughts and ways are higher than ours. God is so good and so awesome; He doesn't stop there. Havilah is just a place of beginning–Hallelujah! Anything that you can accomplish in your own strength is not a "God-sized" assignment and God will not get glory from it. Remember, God is looking for the manifestation of glory so all will know that He is the one, true Living God.

Upon receiving your breakthrough, there is an expansion that takes place. However, bear in mind that the expansion is not to bless your four and no more; it is to do His work and to be His representative in the earth in order to facilitate the restoration of all things. In accordance with Isaiah 54:3, we are purposed to make the desolate places, the places destroyed through sin and death, inhabited and to bring forth restoration–inhabitable lands that are rich and flowing with milk and honey. What God does for us, we are to do for others who do not yet know Him.

This place is a very difficult place to endure; for the time just before the dawn is the darkest time. When your breakthrough is at hand, you feel as though you are at your weakest. It is at that time that God is at His strongest in your life. He will show Himself strong on your behalf like never before. Get ready for the standard to be raised!

Chapter 8

The Third River–Hiddekel:

The name of the third river is Hiddekel which symbolizes the "rapid". It is interesting that this river is only referenced twice in the bible: It appears once in the book of Genesis and again in Daniel 10:4 as it is called "the great river".

God releases greater measures of grace and He also expands our domain, or realm of influence, in a rapid manner. This is where we start seeing the manifestation of the transfer of wealth from the wicked through influence and with authority. Our sphere of influence as "kingdom citizens" is advanced into worldly kingdoms.

> ... *the kingdoms of this world are become [the kingdoms] of our Lord, and of his Christ; and he shall reign for ever and ever. Revelation 11:15*

Daniel, a Jew in bondage in a foreign land, was a high government official in a heathen nation that was not his own. Through his godly influence, God was exalted and praised by a line of heathen kings. This ultimately led to Him using the king of Persia to release the children of Israel to rebuild the temple of God in their own land.

During the releasing of greater measures of grace, God will give you not only rest, but you will also rule in the midst of your enemies.

Chapter 9

The Forth River–Euphrates:

The name of the fourth river is Euphrates which means "fruitfulness" or "that makes fruitful".

> *For the earth bringeth forth fruit of herself; first the blade, then the ear, after that the full corn in the ear.*
> *Mark 4:28*

Do you see the progression of God? The fourth river will bring forth the full fruit, or harvest, of God's purpose in your life. Fruit comes forth to meet the needs of the things that are a part of the system God established through you, thereby causing you to have dominion over the realm He's assigned to you.

Ecosystems that remain in tact provide for every component within the system: food, shelter, and protection–a supply to meet every need. This is, in general terms, God's purpose for us by being His representatives in the earth. We are to be distribution systems to channel supply in order to meet the needs of everything in our domain. That's something to shout about!

Within God's divine plan to restore prosperity to each of us, you can see the pattern of progressive increase which brings us back to the place of fulfilling His command to be fruitful, to multiply, to replenish the earth, to subdue it and to have dominion. As we are shown faithful in executing God's command in the place He sets us, our prosperity is inevitable and greater than we can ever imagine; for He does exceeding abundantly above all that we could ever ask or think, according to the power that works in us (Ephesians 3:20). However, we must have it engrained in every fiber of our being that prosperity will only be accomplished according to His power that we allow to work in us. It can be done no other way.

About the Author

Prophet Valerie Rogers is a member of God Is In Control Church under the leadership of Bishop Elect Rodney S. Walker Sr., an accomplished author and a renowned teacher of prosperity development. Under Bishop Walker, Ms. Rogers received her license to minister, was ordained as an Elder in the Lord's Church, was released into the Office of the Prophet and was set aside as a Prophetic Presbyter within the Another Touch of Glory Covenant Ministries.

Ms. Rogers' greatest desire is to help anyone who desires to walk in true prosperity by helping them establish the proper foundation. She is able to do that for any person that has only a vision and a desire to get started. This is coupled with her passion to impart knowledge and understanding to people who want to get started or who is restarting on the path of a prosperous lifestyle.

She is the President and Chief Executive Officer of Checed Enterprises LLC, a business development firm. She has assisted in developing and establishing small businesses in the United States and its territories. She has successfully assisted in the laying of foundations and establishing business strategies for small businesses and organizations that needed a jump start into the business community and has provided enhanced business plans for established businesses.

Ms. Rogers successfully reestablished businesses needing a new and fresh start, businesses that needed a recovery plan as well as businesses that needed direction in nurturing and bringing to manifestation more than an idea and their zeal to get started. While it is known that most small businesses do not thrive beyond the first few years of being in existence, her keen insight into sound principles helps develop and build business foundations that will last. Her experience also includes helping non-profit organizations accomplish their business goals.

Ms. Rogers is also the founder of Hesed Ministries, a non-profit organization, whose purpose is to show the love and kindness of God to those in need of help emotionally and those who are imprisoned and impoverished; teaching them how to develop and to establish foundations that will bring prosperity into their lives and cause them to be an asset to themselves and to society.

She is a devoted mother of one daughter Nikiyia and one granddaughter Kayla.

That you may know His joy!

OTHER BOOKS SOON TO BE RELEASED

God's Divine Order

Get Rich Thru Your Niche

Establishing the Kingdom – Ruling with Character

Kingdom Release for Prosperity

To contact the author, please write to:

Prophet Valerie Rogers

Checed Publications, LLC

1282 Smallwood Drive West #125

Waldorf, Maryland 20603

Prayer for Salvation

To see the kingdom of God, you must first be born again (John 3:3). Therefore, if you want to fully benefit from the prosperity plan of God, pray this prayer:

> "Heavenly Father, I come to You in the Name of Jesus. Your Word says, *'Whosoever shall call on the name of the Lord shall be saved* (Acts 2:21).' I am calling on You. I pray and ask you, Jesus, to be Lord and King over my life, according to Romans 10:9-10: *'That If thou shalt confess with thy mouth the Lord Jesus, and shalt believe in thine heart that God hath raised him from the dead, thou shalt be saved. For with the heart man believeth unto righteousness; and with the mouth confession is made unto salvation.'* I do that now. I confess that Jesus is Lord, and I believe in my heart that God raised Him from the dead."

Now that you are saved, find a good, word of God preaching and teaching church, and become a part of a church family who will love and care for you as you love and care for them.

Being hooked up to each other increases our strength in God. It's part of His plan for us as the body of the Lord Jesus Christ.